Wild flowers
of the
Cornish hedgerows

Trevor and Endymion Beer

Tor Mark Press • Redruth

The Tor Mark series

Cornish titles
Ancient Cornwall
Birds of Cornwall
Charlestown
China clay, traditional methods
Classic Cornish ghost stories
Classic folk tales from the Land's End
Classic ghost stories from the Land's End
Cornish fairies
Cornish folk-lore
Cornish legends
Cornish mining industry
Cornish mining – underground
Cornish recipes
Cornish saints
Cornish seashore
Cornish smuggling industry
Cornwall's engine houses
Cornwall's railways
Customs and superstitions from Cornish
  folklore
Demons, ghosts and spectres from
  Cornish folklore
Do you know Cornwall?
Down 'long weth we
Exploring Cornwall with your car
Fed fitty
Introducing Cornwall
Jan Bedella's fiddle
Lost ports of Cornwall
Pasty book
Shipwrecks around Land's End

Shipwrecks around the Lizard
Shipwrecks on Cornwall's North coast
Short Cornish dictionary
Story of Cornwall
Story of St Ives
Story of the Cornish language
Story of Truro Cathedral
Strange tales of the Cornish coast
Tales of the Cornish smugglers
Tales of the Cornish wreckers
Twelve walks on the Lizard
Wild flowers of the Cornish coast
Wild flowers of the Cornish hedgerows
1000 Cornish place names

Devonshire titles
Birds of Devon
Classic Devon ghost stories
Devon customs and superstitions
Devon legends
Devon seashore
Devonshire jokes and stories
Shipwrecks of North Devon
Wild flowers of the Devon coast
Wild flowers of the Devon hedgerows

West Country titles
Classic West Country ghost stories
Clotted cream
Pixy book
What shall we do with the smuggled
  brandy?

First published 2000 by Tor Mark Press, PO Box 4, Redruth, Cornwall TR16 5YX
ISBN 0-85025-384-5
© 2000 Trevor and Endymion Beer
All rights reserved
Printed in Great Britain by R Booth (The Troutbeck Press), Mabe, Penryn, Cornwall

Bluebells are plants of hedgerows as well as woodland. In many parts of the county you will also see 'white bluebells', which are actually Three-cornered leeks, Allium triquetrum

Introduction

Cornwall's hedgerows vary greatly in type, from the traditional 'Cornish hedge' (stone walling and earth) to hedgebanks of the Devon style with their broad earth base and dense vegetation. But whether of stone or soil, or a mix of both, all the hedges act as stockproof enclosures, shelters from the vagaries of the weather and homes for wildlife.

This book identifies some of the species of wildflowers to be found in Cornish hedgerows and along the highways and byways associated with them. We have also included their traditional names and a few of the uses to which they have been put over the years. For space reasons we have omitted details of the more obvious plants, including Daisy, Bramble, Dandelion, Snowdrop, Clover and Bluebell.

When you're out and about, keep to footpaths wherever possible and always remember the Country Code. Please leave plantlife for others to enjoy and don't pick or trample the wildflowers or disturb anything else.

Cow/Hedge parsley *Anthriscus sylvestris*
Alternate ferny leaves and erect, furrowed stems growing
80-150cm (32–60in) tall. The delicate scented flowers are lace-
like and white. The flowerhead is branched so that the small
circular clusters of tiny flowers form a larger, loosely circular
flowerhead. Flowers April–June.
Local names: Queen Anne's Lace.
Ancient uses: Used as fodder, often mixed with blackberry tips
and new bracken tops, for pigs. Fed to rabbits as green stuff.
Country children made pea-shooters out of the hollow stems.
Habitat: Hedgerows, woodland margins, roadsides, grassy
places.

Traveller's joy *Clematis vitalba*
A rampant deciduous plant which climbs by twisting its leaf
stalks around the stems of other plants. Like honeysuckle, the
stems become thick and woody with age. The flowers are a
whitish green or cream colour and are fragrantly sweet.
Flowering period July–September.
Local names: Grandfather's whiskers, Old man's beard, Gipsy's
bacca.

Ancient uses: Years ago lengths of the dry stem were smoked. Also rubbed on travellers' bruises to ease aches and pains.
Habitat: Scrub, woodland, old walls, hedgerows.

Wild carrot *Daucus carota*
Growing 50–100cm (20–40in) tall, wild carrot has divided leaves which are fern-like. The stems are erect and often branched. Flowers form on long stems and have lacy heads, with the outer florets being larger than the inner ones. Before the flowers appear the dense greenish heads open to look like miniature birds' nests. Flowers June–August.
Local names: Keggas, Pig's parsley.
Ancient uses: Used against fainting. The wild carrot was dug up and eaten as a vegetable.
Habitat: Hedgebank on railway embankments, rough grassland, roadside verges, waste ground, downs, cliffs, dry meadows.

Above: Traveller's joy
Below: Wild carrot

Herb Robert

Herb Robert *Geranium robertianum*
An annual with hairy stems and leaves which may be green
tinged with red, sometimes completely red. The leaves are fern
shaped and the flowers are pink. It's a strong smelling herb and
grows from 10–50cm (4–20in). Flowering time May–September.
Local names: Bird's eye, Robin's eye, Wren, Bachelor's buttons,
Gipsy flower, Gipsies.
Ancient uses: To treat blood disorders. Leaves were used to
staunch the flow of blood.
Habitat: Hedgebanks, woodlands, old walls, rocks, coasts.

Wall pennywort *Umbilicus rupestris*
Wall pennywort grows between 15–40cm (6–16in) in height.
The larger specimens are usually found in damp shady places. It
is a perennial and flowers June–August. The flowers are small,
bell-shaped, cream or pale greenish-white. The leaves are round
and fleshy. Each leaf has a dimple in the middle where it joins
the stalk.
Local names: Navel wort, Cups-and-saucers, Penny loaves, Penny
pies, Milk-the-cows.
Ancient uses: For cuts, chilblains, inflammation and 'the stone'.
Habitat: Fairly common on walls, dry sandy hedgebanks, rocks
and even among the moss on oak trees.

Above left: Wall pennywort   *Above right: Ragwort*

Ragwort *Senecio jacobaea*
Perennial growing 120cm (4ft) tall, with a rosette of large
divided leaves at the base which often dies before the plant
flowers. Officially a noxious weed, dangerous to horses and
some other livestock, but not usually eaten by animals. It is the
main foodplant of the cinnabar moth, a black and vermillion
day-flying species with black and gold striped larvae. The bright
yellow flowers appear June–October.
Habitat: Hedgerows, roadsides, river embankments, meadows,
pastures, waste land, sand dunes, coastal shingle.

Knapweed *Centaurea nigra*
Perennial with tough, branching stems 30–60cm (1–2ft) high.
Distinguished from thistles by the leaves which are not prickly.
Bright purple flowers found June–September.
Local name: Hardheads.
Ancient uses: Used for wounds and ruptures, bruises, sores and
sore throats. Once used for love divination.
Habitats: Hedgerows, railway embankments, roadsides, scrub,
meadows, grassy places including coastal fields.

Great mullein *Verbascum thapsus*
Great mullein is the largest of the mullein family, growing from
1–2 m ($3^1/_4$–6 ft). It is a biennial and flowers June–August. It has
yellow flowers clustered to form a narrow spike, and large
downy leaves, the whole plant being covered with whitish or
greyish soft hairs.
Habitat: Found on dry soils in sunny places, particularly in
rough dry grassland and waste sites, hedgerows, roadsides,
banks and stony places.

Above left: Great mullein *Above right: Teasel*

Teasel *Dipsacus fullonum*

Growing 1–2m (3¹/₄–6ft) tall, the teasel has a dense rosette of stalked leaves in the first year. In the second year the stiff prickly stems grow erectly with paired, untoothed slender leaves. The flower heads are egg-shaped with a blunt top and a mass of pink, purple or lilac flowers in July–August. The flower bracts underneath are long and spiky.

Ancient uses: The teasing plant of the clothier, it was used for raising the nap on cloth. Rainwater found in the rosette of leaves at the base of the teasel is a good remedy for sore eyes and the same water cures warts.

Habitat: Embankments, hedgerows, roadsides, grassy places, woodland margins, along stream and river banks, waste ground.

Above left: Rosebay willowherb   *Above right: Yellow archangel*

Rosebay willowherb *Chamerion angustifolium*
The long and slender alternate leaves are very slightly toothed, pointed and hairless. The plant grows 80–150cm (32–60in) tall. Flowers (June–September) are deep pink to purple and clustered to form large conical heads.
Ancient uses: A sacred plant never to be picked – in fact the Swiss call it Himmelgraes, Herb of Heaven.
Habitat: Hedgerows, railway embankments, riverbanks, woodland margins, roadsides, fire sites, felled woodland, derelict buildings and waste ground.

Yellow archangel *Lamiastrum galeobdolon*
Grows 30–60cm (12–24in) tall. Strong smelling and hairy, with

paired leaves and leafy runners. The leaves are oval, almost triangular and toothed. The stems are square and the bright yellow flowers (April–July) form in tight whorls up the stem.

Habitat: Hedgerows, woodlands, bushy habitats, coppices, shady places.

Red valerian *Centranthus ruber* (also known as *Valeriana ruber*)

A stout, rather fleshy plant with thick, erect stems 50–80cm (20–32in) in height. The leaves are grey-green or bluish-green, paired and mostly untoothed. Stem leaves are unstalked, oval to spear shaped and have broad bases which clasp the stem. Flowers can be red, pink or white and form in dense fluffy heads. They appear June–August.

Local names: Fowey pride, Ladies needlework, Pride of Padstow, Saucy Bet.

Ancient uses: Very young leaves can be mixed into a lettuce salad or boiled and shaken up with butter. They taste slightly bitter.

Habitat: Stony open hedges, walls, rocks, cliffs, dry sunny sites, sandy places, railways, stony waste ground.

Coltsfoot *Tussilago farfara*

The bright golden flowers (February–April) are daisy-like. The petals are narrow and numerous. The stems are fleshy, stocky and covered in purplish scales. Grows 10–25cm (4–10in) tall. Leaves appear after flowering and are basal, rounded and long-stalked with a heart-shaped base.

Ancient uses: An infusion of leaves can be taken for dry coughs and bronchitis. Beers, jelly and wine for chest complaints are also made from the leaves. Used as a herbal tobacco.

Habitat: Roadsides, hedgebanks, waste ground, cultivated land, embankments, screes, damp sites.

Tufted vetch *Vicia cracca*

A plant with slender, branched stems and alternate leaves which resemble tiny ladders, having 6–15 pairs of narrow leaflets. At the end of each leaf, tendrils twine themselves around vegetation, enabling the plant to climb and clamber some distance. The purplish-blue flowers (June–August) form in long dense heads and are known as pea flowers because they are related to the pea family. The plant grows 80–200cm (32–80in) high.

Above left: Tufted vetch   *Above right: Red campion*

Ancient uses: Used against smallpox and measles.
Habitat: Hedgerows, grassy places, scrub, woodland margins, coastal rocks and shingle, roadsides.

Red campion *Silene dioica*

The leaves are untoothed, oblong to oval, and the lower leaves are stalked. The stems are often branched. A hairy plant, erect, with unscented deep pink flowers, it grows 50–100cm (20–40in) tall and flowers May–November.
Local names: Dolly winter, Fleabites, Red Riding Hood, Bob Robin, Cock Robin, Red Robin, Robin Hood, Robin red breast, Robin's eye, Robin's flower.
Habitat: Deciduous woodland, woodland clearings, hedgebanks, hedgerows, cliff ledges and scree.

Greater bindweed

Calystegia silvatica

A vigorous, hairless plant
with arrow-shaped,
untoothed and stalked
alternate leaves. The stems
are twining and climbing,
and the plant grows up to
3m (10ft) tall. Flowers
(July–September) are large
white trumpets with
yellow centres.

Habitat: Hedgerows, waste-
land, around old buildings
and cultivated land.

Above: Greater bindweed
Below: Yellow fleabane

Yellow fleabane

Pulicaria dysenterica

Densely hairy, the alternate
leaves are greyish under-
neath, heart- or arrow-
shaped and stalked. The
basal leaves are oval with
a narrow base, whilst stem
leaves have clasping stems.
The flowerheads are bright
yellow, daisy-like and form
in clusters. Petals are
numerous and short.

Local name: Harvest flower.

Ancient uses: To deter fleas
and midges.

Habitat: Hedgerows,
ditches, alongside streams,
wet meadows.

Wood anemone

Anemone nemorosa
Grows 5–30cm (2–12in) tall
and in patches. The leaves,
which form in whorls of
three, have 3 deep lobes.
The flowers, which nod in
the slightest breeze, are
usually white, though
sometimes pink or bluish.
Flowers March–May.
Local name: Windflower.
Habitat: Hedgerows, scrub,
woodland, coppices.

Wild basil

Clinopodium vulgare
This plant has square
stems, is slightly aromatic
and is covered in soft hairs.
Grows 40–75cm (16–30in)
tall. The leaves are
opposite and mostly oval.
The deep pink to purple
flowers (July–September)
form in dense whorls at
the base of the upper
leaves.
Habitat: Hedgerows,
scrub, open woodland,
banks, grassy meadows,
dry places.

Greater burdock. Young stalks of this plant, peeled and eaten raw with salt and pepper or boiled in meat broth, were said to increase virility

Greater burdock *Arctium lappa*

A robust and erect plant growing 80–150cm (32–60in) tall. The leaves are alternate. The basal leaves are rough with heart-shaped blades, usually untoothed, and they can grow up to 50cm (20in) long. The flower heads slightly resemble knapweed or thistle heads and are reddish purple, occasionally white. Look for the flower bracts beneath the flower heads. These are golden green with hooked tips. Flowers appear July–September.

Local names: Butter-dock, Cockle-bells, Cockle buttons, Cockle dock, Cuckold dock.

Ancient uses: The leaves were used for wrapping around butter. Also used as a prevention and cure for rheumatism.

Habitat: Hedgerows, waste ground, woodland, clearings.

Ragged robin *Lychnis flos-cuculi*

Slender erect stems which can be branched or unbranched and long slender opposite leaves. Base leaves are oval, spoon-shaped and stalked. Grows 20-70cm (8-28in) tall. Flowers (May–August)

are bright purplish pink. There are four narrow lobes per petal, giving a very ragged look.
Habitat: Wet woodland, marshes, streamsides, damp meadows.

Dog rose *Rosa canina*
A shrub growing about 1–3m (39in-10ft) with hooked prickles. The toothed leaves have 5–7 leaflets which are paired, except for the one on the end which forms the tip of the leaf. The scarlet seed heads or hips form early in autumn. Flowers are pink, sometimes with white centres, and can be found June–July.
Local name: Pig-rose.
Ancient uses: A symbol of the British Monarchy to the present day. Roots were used to cure dog bites. Rosehips, rich in vitamin C, are used to make rosehip syrup, an excellent tonic.
Habitat: Waysides, hedges, woods, open woodland, scrub, woodland margins.

Above: Ragged Robin
Below: Dog rose

Above: Wild arum
Below: Enchanter's nightshade

Wild arum
Arum maculatum
Grows 15–35cm (6–14in) tall. Hairless and fleshy with long stalked, untoothed arrow-shaped leaves which are often covered with dark blotches. The flower is a chocolate brown spike enclosed in a large pointed hood or spathe. The spathe is yellowish-green, some-times streaked or spotted and slightly flushed with purple. Flowers April–May.
Local names: Lords and ladies, Cuckoo pint, Adder's meat, Adder's tongue, Jack-in-the-pulpit, Toad's meat, Wake Robin.
Habitat: Woods, hedgerows, scrub, wooded cliffs, occasionally on cultivated land.

Enchanter's nightshade
Circaea lutetiana
Slender stems with opposite leaves which are stalked and oval with a heart-shaped base and pointed tip. Grows 30–60cm (12–24in) tall.

The flowers (June–August) are white or pinkish and tiny, and they adorn slender, usually branched, stems.

Habitat: Woodland, coppices, shaded places, cultivated land, woodland banks and hedgerows.

Self heal *Prunella vulgaris*
Self heal grows 15–30cm (6–12in) high and is covered with tiny hairs. The flowers are purple or bluish violet, and are clustered in dense, oblong-shaped heads which are pollinated by bees. White or pink flowers (June–November) may occasionally be found. The leaves are slightly stalked, oval to diamond shaped

Self heal

and may be toothed or untoothed. The stem is square and there is a pair of leaves directly under the flower head.

Ancient uses: A wound herb, used to stem blood flow, and also used as an astringent and a tonic. (Self heal is still chosen by modern herbalists as a helpful astringent.)

Habitat: Hedgerows, grassy places, roadsides, open woodlands, woodland tracks and clearings.

Garlic mustard   *Wild strawberry*

Garlic mustard *Alliaria petiolata*
A hairy plant with stiff, slender stems and alternate leaves. The
leaves are heart-shaped, short-stalked, toothed and smell of
garlic when crushed. Flowers are white and clustered, and
appear April–June.
Ancient uses: Used to make a sauce for fish, and as a green or in
salads.
Habitat: Hedgerows, open woodland, waste ground, scrub,
roadsides, wood margins.

Wild strawberry *Fragaria vesca*
The bright green leaves are toothed, stalked and have three
leaflets. The plant is hairy and has slender, erect and branched
flower stems. There are 5 white petals to each yellow centred

flower. Grows 10–25cm (4–10in) tall. Flowers April–July, and
bears the tiny strawberry fruits in late summer.
Ancient uses: The fruit is used to make jam or is eaten fresh with
sugar and cream. Mixed with bramble leaves, the leaves were
given to off-colour or constipated guinea pigs and rabbits.
Habitat: Hedgerows, woodlands, roadsides, embankments,
scrub.

Greater stitchwort *Stellaria holostea*
Grows 30–60cm (12–24in) tall and often forms in patches.
Branched, spreading, straggling stems. Untoothed narrow,
opposite leaves. Belongs to the 'pink' family, so called because
the 5 deeply notched white petals look to have been trimmed
with pinking shears. Flowers April–June.
Local names: Satin flower, Adder's meat, Adder's spit, Lady's
smock, Lady's white petticoats, Old man's shirt, Pisgie or Pixie,
Pisgie flower.
Ancient uses: Used against the 'stitch', a sudden pain or pricking
in the side.
Habitat: Hedgerows, embankments, woodland margins, grassy
places.

Greater stitchwort

Houndstongue   *St John's wort*

Houndstongue *Cynoglossum officinale*
Houndstongue is a biennial and grows up to 40–70cm (16–28in)
high. It is covered in long silky hairs and is soft to touch. The
flowers are blood red to purple and blossom June–August. The
name 'Houndstongue' relates to the shape of the leaves.
Ancient uses: Used for dog bites, burns, baldness, internal sores
and ulcers, skin diseases and piles.
Habitat: Waste ground or by roadsides and hedges, edges of
woods, sand dunes and downs by the sea.

Ivy leaved toadflax, a plant of stony places, both natural and man-made

St John's wort *Hypericum perforatum*

A hairless plant with stiff, erect and branched stems. Leaves are untoothed, unstalked, opposite and oval. Grows 40–80cm (16–32in) tall. Flowers (May–September) are yellow and have 5 petals with many stamens in the centres. They have no nectar.
Ancient uses: To cure catarrh, grow hair, heal cuts and cure sprains. Also used against poisons and to heal burns and, in early cultures, to ward off evil. The plant is named after St John the Baptist.
Habitat: Hedgerows, banks, road verges, woods, scrub, dry fields and other grassy places.

Ivy leaved toadflax *Cymbalaria muralis*

A small trailing plant growing up to 60cm (24in) in length. It has long slender stems adorned with small ivy-shaped leaves. These grow alternately along the stem and are rather fleshy. The flowers (May–September) are tiny snapdragon blossoms of lilac to mauvish violet with a yellow patch on the lower lip.
Local names: Mother of thousands, Mother of millions, Nanny goat's mouth, Roving sailor.
Ancient uses: Introduced in the 17th century to adorn walls of gardens and parks. Now naturalised.
Habitat: Old walls, stony hedgebanks, woods, pavements, rocky places.

Lesser celandine
Ranunculus ficaria
A hairless plant with short fleshy stems and heart-shaped leaves which often bear blotches or spots. It grows 5–25cm (2–10in) high. The flowers (March–May) are bright yellow, starlike and commonly known as 'the first herald of spring'.
Local name: Pilewort.
Ancient uses: Used to treat problems of cows' udders. Heals kernels of the ear and throat (called king's evil). Used also against piles and corns, and effective as a skin cleanser.

Habitat: Hedgerows, damp grassy places, ditches, streams, woodlands.

Wild garlic *Allium ursinum*
A strong smelling, hairless plant with shiny, bright green basal leaves which are fairly broad, fleshy and have a strong smell of garlic when crushed. The flower heads (April–June) are clustered with white star-shaped flowers. The plant grows 25–45cm (10–18in) high.
Local names: Ramsons, Ramsey.
Ancient uses: Country fish sauce was made from the leaves. Bulbs pickled in rum were used against chesty coughs.
Habitat: Hedgerows, deciduous woodlands, scrub, coppices, meadows and banks which are partly shaded.

Wild garlic   *Hemp agrimony*

Hemp agrimony *Eupatorium cannabinum*
The toothed, three-lobed leaves are mostly paired and adorn the
red to purple-tinged, stiff and erect stems. The flowers
(July–September) develop with protruding stamens and are
massed together, forming broad, flat-topped clusters. They are
rarely white, usually pinkish-purple to pink, and they attract
bees and butterflies. The plant grows 90–150cm (36–60in) tall.
Local names: Black elder, Virgin Mary.
Ancient uses: Clears the body of catarrhs and coughs, and helps
with urinary problems and jaundice.
Habitat: Hedgerows, damp woods, pond and river sides,
marshes, ditches, and drier soils in calcareous woods, scrub.

Left: Dog violet

Opposite, top:
Primroses

Opposite, lower:
Honeysuckle

Dog violet *Viola riviniana*

The flowers of the common Dog violet have no scent but are a deep violet blue. Occasionally paler and even white flowers may be found. The leaves have long stalks, and are heart-shaped and gently toothed. The plant grows 8–20cm ($3^1/_2$–8in) tall and avoids wet conditions. Flowering period April–June, although it may flower again at the end of the summer.

Ancient uses: Used against cancer. The juice from boiled violets was also used for headaches.

Habitat: Hedgebanks, open deciduous woodland, grassy places and heaths. Avoids wet conditions.

Primrose *Primula vulgaris*

The primrose has very pale yellow flowers, rarely pink or white. Growing 5–12cm (2–$4^3/_4$in) high, it is soft haired and has flowers on slender stalks January–May. The leaves are bright green, oblong and form rosettes at the base of the plant.

Ancient uses: Used to cure yellow jaundice, skin complaints, ring-worm, burns and scalds.

Habitat: Grassy banks, hedgebanks, open woodland, meadows, ditches and roadsides.

Honeysuckle *Lonicera periclymenum*

A twining deciduous shrub capable of climbing up to 6m (20ft). Pollinated by nocturnal moths, particularly hawk moths, and bumble bees during the day. The flowers (June–October) are creamy white to yellow and often flushed with purple. The opposite leaves are oval to oblong and dark green, and the lower leaves are stalked.

Local names: Woodbine, Woodbind.

Ancient uses: The bark was used to cure jaundice. 'Honeysuckle sticks' were guarantees of good luck. These were hazel sticks where the honeysuckle had entwined itself, the honeysuckle being removed to leave the hazel stick 'twisted' in appearance.

Habitat: Hedgerows, woodlands, coppices, cliffs, rocky places.

Green alkanet   *Common agrimony*

Green alkanet *Pentaglottis sempervirens* (originally Evergreen alkanet and also known as *Anchusa sempervirens*)
Grows 50–100cm (20–40in) tall. A bristly, leafy, erect plant with branched stems. Leaves are untoothed, have a narrow base and are oval to spear shaped. Flowers (April–July) are bright blue, spiralled and clustered.
Local name: Bird's eye.
Ancient uses: Roots produce a red dye.
Habitat: Shaded hedgebanks, damp woodland, borders, grassy and waste places. Often found growing near buildings.

Common agrimony

Agrimonia eupatoria

A gracefully slender plant growing 50–100cm (20–40in) tall. Hairy, with erect stems and a slender spike of yellow flowers (June–August). Each tiny flower has 5 petals. Leaves are alternate and toothed, and there are 3–6 main pairs of leaflets to each.

Local name: Salt-and-pepper.

Ancient uses: Against snake bites, dysentery and liver problems. Agrimony wine is used for colds; agrimony tea is good as a tonic.

Habitat: Hedgerows, wood edges, grassy verges and railway embankments.

Germander speedwell

Germander speedwell *Veronica chamaedrys*

The bright blue flowers are quite small, measuring 9-12mm ($^3/_8$in) across, and they each have two stamens. The oval leaves are almost triangular, the lower ones having short stalks – unlike the upper leaves which are usually unstalked. The plant grows 20-40cm (8-16in) tall and is pollinated by small flies. Flowers March–July.

Local names: Mother-breaks-her-heart, Cat's eyes.

Ancient uses: Was used as a cure for jaundice and, in the form of a tea, for indigestion and pains in the stomach.

Habitat: Hedgerows, embankments, grassy areas, road and lane verges, woodland borders, damp stony ground.

Above left: Pignut   *Above right: Hedge woundwort*

Hedge woundwort *Stachys sylvatica*

Grows 60–100cm (24–40in) tall. Has square, erect stems and is softly hairy. The paired leaves with short stalks are coarsely toothed, narrow to broadly heart-shaped and pointed (rather like nettle leaves). The basal leaves are long-stalked. Spikes of flowers (June–September) are dull reddish-purple, with whorls forming at the base of the upper leaves.

Habitat: Hedgerows, roadsides, waste ground, woodland.

Pignut *Conopodium majus*

Grows 20–40cm (8–16in) tall. Has very fine fern feather-like leaves which are alternate and divided. The flowers are white, delicate, lace-like and form in loose umbels. Umbels have 6–12 main spokes. An erect plant which flowers May–July.

Local names: Earthnut, Varenut, Fern-nut, Grovenut, Killimore, Underground nut.

Ancient uses: The 'nuts' found under the plant tubers can be eaten either raw after scraping or peeled and boiled in broth. Attempts were made in the past to cultivate this plant, but these failed because it will not grow in tilled soil.

Habitat: Hedgerows, open woodlands, banks, roadsides, rough grassy places, heaths.

Foxglove *Digitalis purpurea*

Growing 1–2m (3¹/₄–6ft) tall, the Foxglove is an erect, leafy plant covered in soft hairs. The leaves are broad, blunt, finely toothed and soft grey-green underneath. Flowers (June–September) are large, drooping bells, pink to purple with dark spots surrounded by white rings inside each one.

Local names: Cowflop, Cowslip, Flop-a-dock, Flop poppy, Green pops, Green poppies, Pop dock, Pop-glove, Poppy, Poppy-dock, Scabbit-dock.

Ancient uses: In 1785 William Withering discovered that the Foxglove was a good diuretic and that digitalis (found in the leaves) was a major instrument against heart disease.

Habitat: Hedgebanks, wood margins, lane verges, river banks, scrub, open heathland, rocky hillsides.

Index